AFRICAN PRAYERS

PRAISE
THANKSGIVING
HOPE AND
TRUST

ROBERT
VAN DE WEYER

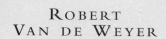
AFRICAN
PRAYERS

PRAISE
THANKSGIVING
HOPE AND
TRUST

DIMENSIONS
FOR LIVING
Nashville

INTRODUCTION

In the late nineteenth and early twentieth centuries, a small number of European missionaries and settlers took the trouble to study native African culture, learning the languages and listening to the people. They invariably found within that culture a strong and vibrant religion, which expressed itself in worship, prayers, and stories. Happily they recorded what they saw and heard — and the prayers contained in this book are taken from those records.

One of the most striking features of almost all the tribal religions of Africa is their belief in a supreme divine being. Of course, each tribe has a different name for the supreme divinity; but it is quite legitimate to translate all these names with the single word "God." They may have been influenced by their intermittent contact, over many centuries, with both Christian and Muslim traders and preachers. But it seems more likely that the sense of God is inherent within the human soul. Indeed, were this not so, it is impossible to understand how Christianity took root so quickly in Africa during the twentieth century, and now flourishes so luxuriantly.

Thus, if you read this book as a Christian, you are encountering religions that, like the Judaism of the Old Testament, know God but do not yet know his fullness in Christ. And regardless of your present faith, you may read this book as a witness to spiritual truths, which are shared by all humanity.

1

DAYS AND YEARS

Before Dawn

Wake us, God, before dawn has broken, that we may prepare ourselves for work. And as we go out to our fields, protect us from the wild animal and the venomous serpent, from the sharp stone and the falling rock.

Konde, Tanzania

A Good Night and a Good Day

At dawn, O God, I thank you for the good night you have given me, and ask you to give me a good day.
At dusk, O God, I thank you for the good day you have given me, and ask you to give me a good night.

Galla, Ethiopia

Constant Prayer

O God, incline your ear to us, and listen to our constant prayer. Even if you are weary, hear our pleas. Protect our children and livestock. When your light is shrouded by the cloak of night, and your glory cannot be seen, remain close to us. When the sun is shining in the sky, and we can see the beauty of your creation, be kind to us. Grant success to all our work; do not thwart us in anything we try to do. Do not drive away the spirits of our ancestors, but let them watch over us.

Nandi, Kenya

As the sun sets

Father, as the sun sets I turn to you
in trust. I know that you will protect
me through the night. I know that
you will never leave me unguarded.

Dinka, Sudan

The new moon

Every month the moon dies; may
the sin within me die with the
moon. Every month the moon is
reborn; may the goodness within me
be reborn with the moon.

Bushmen, South Africa

The year's end

The year's end comes to meet us. We
give thanks to you, O God, that
misfortune has passed us by, so that
we have been free from illness and
injury. Thus we sit together in peace,
as we sat together a year ago.

Aro, Sierra Leone

The new year

*May the coming year bring us joy and
happiness.*
*Let our boys grow into strong young
men, and our young men maintain their
strength.*
*Let our pregnant women safely give
birth, and our new mothers provide
ample milk for their children.*
*Let travellers reach the end of their
journeys, and those at home be protected
from storm and violence.*
*Let the sheep feeding on the hills return,
and all the cows have calves.*
*Let people and livestock alike enjoy
good health.*

Mensa, Ethiopia

A WOMAN'S MORNING PRAYER

Morning has risen.
O God, take away from our heads
the sleepiness of the night, and from
our limbs the sleepiness of the
night.
During this day protect us from
every kind of ill and misfortune that
we may return safely home at night.

Pygmies, Zaire

TO THE SUN

*O sun, as you rise in the east through
God's power, I ask you to burn away all
the evil thoughts that have entered my
mind during the night.*
*O sun, as you rise to the top of the sky
through God's power, I ask your warmth
to fill my heart with feelings of kindness
and generosity towards others.*
*O sun, as you fall to the west through
God's power, I ask that your soft
evening rays may make me calm and
content, that I may sleep in peace.*

Abaluyia, Kenya

To the moon

O moon, as you wax through God's power, I ask that our children may grow in strength and dexterity, that they may perform well the tasks of adulthood.

O moon, as you wane through God's power, I ask that our old people may decline in strength and dexterity with grace and without resentment, that they may become wise and content.

Abaluyia, Kenya

To the stars

O stars, as you come out at dusk through God's power, I ask that your beauty may fill our dreams, so that all the thoughts of the night may be good and happy. O stars, as you go in at dawn, I ask that the memory of your beauty may remain in our minds, that all the thoughts of the day may be good and happy.

Abaluyia, Kenya

To the trees

O trees, as your leaves grow on your branches by God's power, I ask that our young men and women may be vigorous and strong, enjoying both their work and recreation to the full. O trees, as your leaves fall from your branches by God's power, I ask that our old men and women may be content to die when their lives are complete.

Abaluyia, Kenya

2

LIFE AND HEALTH

Clinging to life

We come to you, O God, to ask for life. Help us to cling to life. We know that you are strong, and so we put our trust in you. Hasten to help us. Those whom you help will gather shells from the seashore, to make gifts for you.

Fang, Cameroon

A sick wife

O God, you have ordained that a man should marry a woman; and you forge a bond of love between them. You caused me to marry this woman, whom I love with all my heart. I beg you to heal her of the illness from which she now suffers. Come to her help, and make her well.

Fang, Cameroon

The mystery of sickness

Father, you live in heaven above and on the earth below. You created all things, and you see all things. We are your little children. Why do some of us fall sick? Is sickness the consequence of our sin? Or do you inflict sickness upon us to test our faith in you? If this child is sick because I have sinned, punish me alone. If you are testing my faith, make my body suffer instead.

Luguru, Tanzania

A sick child

O God, you are great. You created me and all my family. I have no one to turn to but you. Look down from heaven upon my child, who is sick. You know how much I desire my child to be healed. Grant my desire.

Anuak, Sudan

A SICK SON

God of our ancestors, God of my father and mother, I have broken none of your commandments. I have chopped firewood in the rain for my relatives. When I have killed an animal, I have given every part to them, keeping back nothing for myself. Now my son is sick and weak. Remember my innocence, and reward me for my goodness; heal him, and make his body strong again.

Ngombe, Zaire

CLEANSING THE SKIN

I have lit a fire for you, O God. I have given you my strongest beer and my finest food. While you bask in my light and take pleasure in my beer and food, I shall prepare my child for you. I shall dress him in beautiful robes, and I shall teach him songs to sing to you. Then I shall invite you into his hut. When you see him and hear him, I beg you to come close and lay your hand upon him. In this way you will cleanse him of the rash that now destroys his skin. After you have cleansed him, I shall teach him to be your most faithful servant, performing whatever deeds you may demand of him. I promise that you will never regret what you have done for him.

Banyankore, Uganda

AN EPIDEMIC

*A fever is spreading through our people.
We, the elders, have gathered to speak to
you, O God of our ancestors. What have
our people done to deserve this suffering?
What have our children done, that they
too should be struck down? There are
not enough people who are well, to
nurse those who are ill. There are not
enough people who remain strong, to
fetch water for those crying out with
thirst. What sins have we committed, to
bring upon ourselves this calamity? We
offer you our food; give us our health.*

Chewa, Malawi

THE POWER OF MEDICINES

I have given my medicines to this
man; but without your power, they
are worthless. May my medicines be
the means by which you enter this
man and make him well.

Meru, Kenya

THE PHYSICIAN'S TASK

People trust me to heal them. Stand
behind me when I examine those
who are sick, that I may discern
their sickness correctly. Stand beside
me when I choose which medicine
to administer, that I may provide the
cure. Stand in front of me when
sickness must lead to death, that I
may speak words of comfort.

Ashanti, Ghana

THE HEALER'S CALL

Spirit of God, for you all things are possible. Without you, I can do nothing. When my people called me to be a healer, I entrusted myself to your power; to you I consecrated my soul. Every day I wonder whether their call was your call; every day I fear that my efforts will be fruitless. Acknowledge that call, and quell my fears.

Fang, Cameroon

GOOD FORTUNE

Let me smile with gratitude when good fortune befalls me. Let me never become proud, imagining that good fortune is the reward for my virtue and goodness. Let me never become complacent, imagining that good fortune will always be my lot. Let me never cease to enjoy good fortune when it occurs. And let me share my good fortune with others.

Banyankore, Uganda

DIVINE CONTROL

O God, you gave us life; by your will we remain alive; and at the time of your choosing we shall die. Thank you for giving us life; may our time on earth be happy and healthy; and may death be peaceful.

Dinka, Sudan

TO ANCESTORS

*May our ancestors receive our gifts of
wine and corn in a spirit of gratitude;
and in their gratitude, may they protect
and defend us from all danger and
misfortune.*
*May our ancestors take pride in our
conduct, knowing that we are following
the ancient customs that they passed on
to us; and in their pride may they bless
us with good health and fortune.*

Meru, Kenya

SUPERNATURAL POWER

O God, you are great and mighty.
You are the one who created me
and my family; you are the one who
sustains and feeds us. You are the
most powerful of all supernatural
powers. Now one of my children is
sick. No natural power can cure my
child, and I fear that my child may
die. Use your supernatural power to
heal my child – and I beg you to do
it quickly.

Nuer, Sudan

Cleansing from sickness

If you are truly divine, cleanse this
woman of the terrible sickness that besets
her.
Cleanse her blood of the impurities that
corrupt it.
Cleanse her breast of the phlegm that
chokes it.
Cleanse her brain of the mist that
darkens it.
Cleanse her skin of the soreness that
reddens it.
And cleanse her soul of the evil that is
the source of the illness.

Dinka, Sudan

An epidemic

You promised our ancestors that
you would keep us healthy; but now
an epidemic has beset us. Men,
women, and children are falling ill,
their skin turning sore and their
flesh wasting away. You have broken
your promise. Will any of our
people survive, or will all die?
Renew your promise – and keep it.

Meru, Kenya

3

BIRTH AND DEATH

ASKING FOR SONS AND DAUGHTERS

*I wish my wife to bear children; grant
children to my wife, O God.
If I were to die tomorrow, I should have
no heirs; grant children to her soon,
O God.
If she bears a son, I shall give him the
name of my grandfather; grant a son to
my wife, O God.
If she bears a daughter, I shall give her
the name of my grandmother; grant a
daughter to my wife, O God.
Would it displease you, O God, if my
wife bore many children, so our home
was filled with the sound of their voices?
Grant children to my wife, O God.*

Giur, Sudan

A DAY OF BIRTH

Hail the day on which this child is
born. Our joy is overflowing. We
sing your praises, O God, that this
woman has safely delivered a tiny
infant. This is the day for which she
and her husband have yearned. We
shall remember this day as a day of
gratitude and hope.

Masai, Kenya

A FATHER'S PLEA

All our ancestors, all who lived here
in the near past and the distant past,
be my witnesses: I plead with you,
O God, to let this child be safely
born. If I have sinned against you,
be merciful; and if you cannot be
merciful, punish me as I deserve –
even slay me. All I ask is that my
wife gives birth to my child – and
that my wife and child are healthy.

Mende, Sierra Leone

A MIDWIFE'S PLEA

*O God, do not let this woman fall sick,
and do not let her weaken. I have given
her a bed on which to lie and a pillow
on which to rest her head. Now I ask
you to help her in her task and sustain
her in her pain.*

Akim-Kotoku, Ghana

POWER OVER DEATH

*God, you are deathless; your power is
greater than the power of death. God,
you live forever; you will never feel the
cold sleep that is the destiny of all whom
you have created. Give a fragment of
your power to these children, so they
may defy all danger and sickness,
surviving until the decay of old age
overcomes them.*

Fang, Cameroon

WELCOMING GOD IN THE HOME

You have come into our home, O
God, and we welcome you. Stay
with us, and look after our children.
Keep them safe and well. Show
them the skills that they must
practise in adulthood. Teach them to
honor us, their parents, and to abide
strictly by the customs of our
people.

Lango, Uganda

HOPING FOR TWINS

You alone can create twins; you are
their real Father. I ask you to
impregnate my wife with twins. I
offer you my finest bull in return.

Dinka, Sudan

A GIRL'S PUBERTY

*You, O God, are our Father; upon you
all people depend. You are our Mother;
to you all people are devoted. You are
the Spirit within us; through you, all
people know what is right and wrong.
You have given us this daughter as a
gift; and now she has reached puberty.
Do not let her menstruate to no
purpose; may her bleeding contain the
promise of fertility, that in the fullness of
time she may bear many children.*

Ashanti, Ghana

A BABY'S DEATH

O Mother, who dwells in heaven,
we thank you for the brief life of
this baby. Now that you have taken
this baby to your home above the
sky, we ask you to give us a new
baby in exchange. And may the new
baby live through childhood and
adulthood, to the ripeness of old
age.

Ashanti, Ghana

TOO SOON FOR DEATH

I wish, O God, you had not come
today; you have called too soon. I
am not yet ready to die; I have too
much left to do. Let me eat food
and drink water, and let a fire be lit
beside me, that I might regain my
strength. Return to heaven, and call
again at a later date.

Ovambo, Namibia

The end of life

There are people who hate me, and whom I have hated; yet now I reach the end of my life, I have only love for them. I forgive all the wrongs that others have done to me; and I ask others to forgive the wrongs that I have done to them. Above all, O God, I confess that I have sinned against you, and I beg your forgiveness. Have mercy upon me, and love me.

Dinka, Sudan

The death of a parent

O great God, you have made all that is good. Yet you have brought great sorrow to us with the death of our beloved parent. You should have planned the world in such a way that human beings are not subject to death, and so do not suffer the pain of bereavement. O God, great sadness overwhelms us.

Ovambo, Namibia

The death of a husband

My husband has abandoned me; he has gone and will never return. I am lost; all joy has drained from my life. He fetched water and chopped firewood for me. He clothed me in fine robes and provided fine food for me to cook. Why has he left me? What shall I do now? O God, I look to you for help, and to you alone.

Basoga, Uganda

Burying a loved one

The gates of life have closed, and the gates of death are opening. The spirits of departed ancestors are gathering at the grave to welcome our loved one. They are thronging together, like mosquitoes at night swarming around a lamp, or like dead leaves whirling in the wind. We have said: "Farewell." And our loved one has gone. The spirits call out: "Come." And our loved one comes. Dear God, we know that you are watching over this journey from life to death, which our loved one is making; keep our loved one safe, that death may bring peace and contentment.

Hottentot, South Africa

Parents' death

When my father died, I was not only filled with grief, but I felt lost, because he could no longer guide me. When my mother died, I was not only filled with grief, but I felt lonely, because she could no longer comfort me. I continue to mourn my father and mother; but through their deaths, O God, you have taught me to trust in you for guidance and comfort.

Nama, South Africa

Death before birth

When the old year meets the new year, death meets birth. At that moment, O God, you teach us that oldness comes before newness, and death comes before birth. Let the old ways of sin and corruption die, and new ways of goodness and purity be born.

Nandi, Kenya

BEGINNING AND END

The day is like a circle, starting at dawn and ending at dawn. The year is like a circle, starting on the shortest day and ending at the shortest day. Life too is like a circle, beginning with helplessness and ending with helplessness. Just as the end of a day is the beginning of a new day, and just as the end of a year is the beginning of a new year, so the end of a life is the beginning of a new life. We thank you, O God, for the passing of time.

Abaluyia, Kenya

THE DEATH OF A HUSBAND

My husband has abandoned me. He was my most devoted friend, and now he has gone. He was my partner in all that I do, and he has passed on to the other world. He was the devoted father to my children, and he will now be absent forever. How can I live without him? O God, I want to die, and yet my children need me to live. Take away the pain of my grief, that I may be a good mother once again.

Ngombe, Zaire

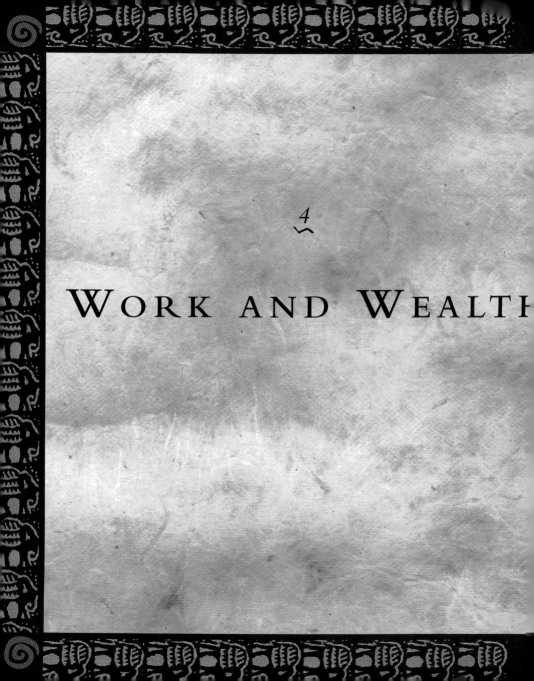

4

WORK AND WEALTH

DIVINE GIFTS

O God, you have given me my herds.
The meat that I eat, and the milk that I
drink, are gifts from your hand. All
cattle belong to you, and you entrust
them to people as you think fit. O God,
you have given me my fields and
streams. The bread that I eat, and the
water that I drink, are gifts from your
hand. All land belongs to you, and you
entrust it to people as you think fit. O
God, you have given me my sons and
daughters. The boys whom I cherish, and
the girls whom I love, are gifts from your
hand. All children belong to you, and
you entrust them to people as you think
fit.

Zulu, South Africa

THE STRENGTH TO WORK

You, O God, are the creator of all.
Today, we, your children, prostrate
ourselves before you. In ourselves
we have no strength; all our strength
comes from you. In themselves, our
seeds have no power to grow; all
their power comes from you. Give
us strength to sow the seeds; give
them power to grow; and give us
strength to harvest the crop.

Lozi, Zambia

THE DAY FOR SOWING

We greet you, Father, this bright morning. We believe that this is the day you have chosen, when we should sow our millet. Make it germinate. May at least eight seeds out of nine sprout. Let this be a happy year. Give a wife to the man who is single. Give a child to the woman who is barren. Protect everyone against thorns and snakes. Pour out the rain, as we pour water from a pot, that the rivers may fill and the grain swell.

Dogun, Mali

THANKS FOR THE HARVEST

The edges of the year have met; we have gathered the harvest, and soon we shall be sowing once more. I take the finest of my new yams and offer them to you, O God. I thank you for the harvest, and I ask you to bless the sowing.

Ashanti, Ghana

FOOD AND DRINK

From our harvest we bake bread; and when we eat the bread, we gain strength to plough our fields. From our cattle we take milk; and when we drink the milk, we gain energy to tend our herds. May our harvests always be plentiful, and our cattle always be healthy.

Nandi, Kenya

SUCCESS IN HUNTING

In which parts of the forest can I
hunt with success, O God? In
which parts of the forest have you
prepared birds and animals for me
to kill? Guide me to the places that
you have ordained, and point my
arrows at the creatures that you
have chosen.

Zande, Sudan

EARTH, TREES, AND STREAMS

*Wherever my people dig, may your earth
be kind to them; when they entrust their
seeds to the earth, may the soil in that
place be fertile. Wherever my people seek
wood, may your trees fall easily under
their axes; when they cut the trunks into
the shapes they require, may the wood
be soft to the chisel. Wherever my people
go for water, may your streams be full
and clear; when they quench their thirst,
may the taste of the water be sweet.
May your earth, your trees, and your
streams express your love for your sons
and your daughters.*

Didinga, Sudan

SUCCESS IN FISHING

O Spirit of creation, may the wind fall, so that the lake is calm. Then I can paddle my canoe swiftly, and steer it easily, to the place where the fish swim.

Luguru, Tanzania

LEARNING TO HUNT AND FISH

You have ordained, O God, that the antelope should leap; in the same way you have ordained that humans should hunt and fish. The adult antelope teaches its young to leap; in the same way I teach my children to hunt and fish.

Lobi, Ivory Coast

COMPLETING THE DAY'S WORK

May the sun be slow to set today. Hold the sun in the sky that I may complete my work before dark.

Zande, Sudan

For the best

When my work is going well, O
God, I thank you; and when my
work is going badly, I ask you for
help. I cannot tell whether you
acknowledge my gratitude; but I
offer it anyway. I know that
sometimes you answer my requests,
and sometimes you do not; but I
trust that you always act for the
best.

Nandi, Kenya

Between sowing and reaping

*When we sow our seeds, O God, we
ask you to be generous to us. When we
have reaped the harvest, we thank you
for being generous to us. And between
sowing and reaping, we must trust in
your generosity. Forgive us for finding it
so hard to trust in you, especially when
the weather is unfavorable.*

Chewa, Malawi

CATCHING FISH

You make the sea rise and fall. You provide the sea with water from the high mountains and from the sky. You fill the sea with fish of every kind, and we watch them darting to and fro. And you have made these fish good to eat. So when we try to catch the fish, draw the fish towards us that our work may be easy.

Lobi, Ivory Coast

HUNTING WILD ANIMALS

You have filled the land with animals, and you have put flesh on their bones. You have made our teeth sharp and our jaws strong, so that we can chew this flesh; and you have made our tongues crave the taste of meat. Our teeth, our jaws, and our tongues form a promise made by you to us, that you will provide us with enough meat to sustain us. We ask you to keep your promise when we go out hunting each morning.

Ila, Zambia

5

CONFLICT AND TROUBLE

CALL TO WAR

We were resting at home when a
messenger came from our chief,
calling us to war. So we come to
you, O God, to ask you to march at
our head, leading our advance. In
our homeland there is no forest
where our people can hide. So we
ask you to surround our
homesteads, protecting our families
while we are away. You, O God, are
our leader and our protector.

Ewe, Ghana

A JUST CAUSE

*I pick up the spear used by my father,
and his father, and his father's father;
and I march toward the battle. May my
feet not stumble, and may my arms be
strong. The cause is just: the enemy has
slain my brother, my cousin, and my
father's father. May today be the day
when their deaths are avenged.*

Giur, Sudan

FREEDOM FROM OPPRESSION

*Dear God, the moon and the stars move
freely across the sky; now through your
power we are free. You made our feet
swift and our arms strong, enabling us to
cast off the tribe that has oppressed us.
Once again our own chiefs rule over us,
and our own customs guide our actions.*

Dinka, Sudan

Marching towards the enemy

May we pour down upon our enemy like a mighty torrent. Let us be like a river in full flow, after rain has fallen on the mountains. Just as the water hisses over the hot sands, so may our feet hiss as we march towards the foe. As the swirling water tears up every tree and shrub in its path, so may we tear apart every warrior that fights against us.

Didinga, Sudan

The pride of victory

You, O God, ordered our attack and guided our spears; we thank you for giving us victory. As our women winnow grain, dividing the chaff from the wheat, so we have winnowed our enemies, dividing the warriors from their weapons. As our women cast aside the chaff, allowing it to be blown away by the wind, so we have scattered those warriors, allowing them to flee to their homes. As our women keep the grain, baking bread to eat, so we have kept their weapons, storing them for future battles. In their villages the warriors tear their hair at the humiliation of defeat, and the women and children mock them for their weakness and cowardice. In our villages we dance with the pride of victory, and our women and children cheer us for our strength and valour.

Didinga, Sudan

THE BITTERNESS OF DEFEAT

O God, you have deserted us and gone over to our enemies. Their arrows flew swiftly through the air and pierced the flesh of our finest young men; our arrows fell to the ground and were trampled underfoot. Now our villages are filled with the cries of young widows and fatherless children; and the villages of our enemies are filled with songs of praise and joy. Will you give us the sweet taste of revenge? Or must we endure the bitter taste of defeat forever?

Banyarwanda, Ruanda

DEMONIC POWERS

Help us, Father, to discern those men and women in our midst who possess demonic powers – who cause innocent children to fall sick, pregnant women to miscarry, cattle to go dry, and crops to fail. And when we have discerned such men and women, give us courage to confront them. If they allow our priests to cleanse them, then we shall be merciful; but if they defy our priests, we shall kill them.

Bakuba, Zaire

THE IRONY OF FAMINE

At this time of famine, who is laughing? The ants are laughing. As our people die, who takes possession of their homes? The ants take possession of their homes. O God, why have you allowed the human being to be humiliated by the tiny ant?

Dinka, Sudan

FLEEING FROM FAMINE

*Famine is upon us. We have no millet,
maize, or beans. Our cattle, sheep, and
goats are dying for lack of water and
grass. Our chickens lie lifeless on the
ground. The breasts of nursing mothers
are dry, and their children cry with
hunger. So we have decided to leave our
village, in the hope of finding a place
where the rivers flow and the trees are
heavy with fruit.
O God, if you want us to survive, lead
us to such a place.*

Lobi, Ivory Coast

THE MYSTERY OF FAMINE

You have turned against us, O God.
You, who created the sun, destroy us
by driving away the clouds that
bring rain. You have forsaken us, O
God. You, who created the moon,
stand aside while our crops wither
and livestock dies. Why have you
turned against us? Why have you
forsaken us?

Dinka, Sudan

THE CAUSE OF MISFORTUNE

O ancestors, are you the cause of
our misfortune. Are you causing our
crops to fail, our livestock to fall
sick, and our wells to dry up? Are
you causing our women to become
barren, our young men to fall sick,
and our old people to talk
nonsense? Or should we blame
God, who created us all?

Abaluyia, Kenya

The mystery of suffering

Why are you punishing me, O God? Why are you making my children fall sick and my crops fail? If I were to meet you face to face, I should demand an answer. Why do you not bless me, as you bless others? Why do you not keep my children well and make my harvest plentiful? If I were to meet you face to face, I should fight you with my spear.

Banyarwanda, Ruanda

After defeat

Our nation has been defeated in war. Our finest and strongest young men have been cut down on the field of battle. Young wives have become widows, young virgins are destined to grow old as virgins, babies will grow up without fathers. And our pride has been shattered. O God, give our enemies the generosity to make peace with us, that our suffering may not grow worse. And give us the wisdom never to make war again.

Meru, Kenya

Days of Old

Once our people were good.
Husbands were faithful to their
wives, and wives cherished their
husbands. Children obeyed their
parents, and parents encouraged
their children. Old people spoke
with wisdom, and young people
listened with respect. Now husbands
betray their wives, and wives treat
their husbands with contempt.
Children mock their parents, and
parents care little for their children.
And old people are ignored.
Restore the days of old, O God;
restore the days that I remember
from long ago.

Bakuba, Zaire

Neither Sun Nor Rain

Have you forsaken us, O God?
The sun refuses to shine; its bright rays
are constantly covered with cloud. Yet the
clouds refuse to give rain; they never
turn from white to grey and black. So
the crops, lacking both sun and rain,
refuse to grow.
Have you forsaken us, O God; or have
you decided that we should starve to
death?

Dinka, Sudan

6

FAITH AND TRUST

GOD'S CARE AND PROTECTION

*Everlasting God, who has existed from
before the beginning of time, listen to us.
Everlasting God, who is older than the
oldest mountain or river, look at us.
Everlasting God, who carries the world
in his hands, take care of us.
Everlasting God, who has fashioned the
beauty of the horse, protect us.*

Galla, Ethiopia

POSTURE FOR PRAYER

*I call upon God, the Father of all our
fathers. I spread out the palms of my
hands in prayer. You who created the
earth and all living beings, listen to me.
You who send rain from the sky, have
mercy on me. I trust in you for all
things.*

Shilluk, Sudan

SPEAKING THE TRUTH

Though the whole tribe has turned
against me, I shall not fear. Though
the tribe holds a feast to dishonor
me, I shall not be anxious. I have
spoken the truth and acted rightly;
so you, O God, are with me.

Dinka, Sudan

READY FOR GOD

You have turned against us, O God,
because our words and actions have
made you angry. But you will not
reject us forever; you will not kill
us, nor will you punish us more
than we can bear. Soon you will
turn your face toward us once more
and invite us to speak and act
according to your laws. When that
moment comes, we shall be ready.

Dinka, Sudan

USELESS SACRIFICES AND RITUALS

Great God, why do you refuse to hear us? Why will you not listen to our pleas? We have offered many sacrifices to you, and we have honored you with numerous rituals. Yet when we ask for rain, the skies remain clear. When we ask you to heal our sick children, their sickness worsens. When we ask you to make our barren women pregnant, their wombs remain empty. Tell us what we must do to win your favor, and we shall do it.

Dinka, Sudan

GOD'S CONSTANT PRESENCE

I pray to you in the busy hours of the day and in the quiet hours of the night. I thank you for sustaining my family and me; every evening I praise you for keeping us alive and healthy for another day. When I walk through the high grass to my cattle, I know that you walk with me. When I lie down to sleep in my hut, I know that you lie beside me. When I eat my meals at dawn and at dusk, I know that you have provided the food. You are constantly present, and I am constantly aware of your presence. Yes, I pray to you at every hour of the day and night.

Shilluk, Sudan

A DISOBEDIENT SON

Here is my son, O God. I labored to feed him. I trained him, showing him all the skills that a man should know. I taught him the customs and traditions of our people. Yet now, when he is old enough to work for me, he refuses. He prefers to spend his day playing with his friends, and his nights drinking beer, than to do the tasks that I require. What should I do? Should I stop feeding him? Should I throw him out of my house, so that he must fend for himself? Or should I be patient, waiting for him to see the error and folly of his ways? I am utterly perplexed and need your guidance.

Mende, Sierra Leone

NEEDING FORGIVENESS

I beg forgiveness. In anger I have killed an animal that belonged to a neighbor. My neighbor had said something rude about my family; and the following night, I went out and slew his finest bull. I ask you, O God, to forgive this wicked act. I also ask you to guide me. Should I confess to my neighbor what I have done and thereby risk his taking revenge on my family? Or should I remain quiet in the hope that he does not suspect my guilt?

Bambara, Mali

THE SOURCE OF LIFE

You, Father, are the source of life.
You created all living beings; and
without your constant care, every
living being would die. You give
energy to all living beings; and
without your constant care, every
living being would lie motionless
on the ground. You send rain and
sunshine alternately from the sky,
causing our crops to grow. When
there are conflicts within families
and between families, you soften
people's hearts and restore peace.
And when people die, you embrace
them and make them your children.

Nuer, Sudan

BEING BORN AGAIN

*God, at the time when you made the
earth, you also created the sun; at dawn
the sun is born, at dusk it dies, and at
dawn it is born again. At the time when
you made the sun, you also created the
moon; at the start of the month the
moon starts to grow, in the middle of the
month it starts to shrink, and at the end
it starts to grow again. At the time when
you made the moon, you also created the
stars; at dusk the stars are born, at dawn
they die, and at dusk they are born
again. At the time when you made the
stars, you also created human beings;
they are born, and some years later they
die. Are they born again? This, O God,
is the question that we constantly ask
and that you never answer.*

Dinka, Sudan

DIVINE JUDGMENT

We are in constant danger from your wrath, O God. If we incur your disapproval, you may curse us. If we offend you, you may punish us. So why do people not fear you and obey you? Why do they not strive for your approval? Why do they not use all their strength to cause you pleasure? Do not curse or punish me for the sins of my neighbors; judge me on my merits alone. I shall always act in a manner that you will call righteous.

Konde, Tanzania

IN THE BEGINNING

In the beginning God was. Today God is. Tomorrow God will be. Who has seen God and knows his form? No one, because he has no body in himself; our arms and legs are the limbs with which he moves. Who has heard God and knows his tone? No one, because he has no voice in himself; our conscience is the mouth by which he speaks. Who has drawn close to God, and felt his warmth? No one, because he is beyond all reach; our hearts are the means by which he loves.

Pygmies, Zaire

You and us

Look at us, O God. You are very
old because you created our original
ancestor; but we are very young.
You are very wise because you
created the whole world; but we are
very foolish. You are very good
because you cherish and sustain all
that lives; but we are often wicked.
You are very strong because you
turn the calm air into a raging
storm; but we are weak and frail.

Galla, Ethiopia

Turning away

*Sometimes we turn our backs on you, O
God. We forget that you exist, and we
ignore your laws. But when our backs
are turned toward you, terrible
misfortune befalls us. Sometimes you
turn your backs on us, O God. You
forget that we exist, and you ignore our
needs. But when your back is turned
toward us, terrible misfortune besets us.
Let us always face one another, O God.*

Shilluk, Sudan

Parent, creator, master, and intelligence

*We are your children, O God, and you
are our father and mother. We are your
creatures, O God, and you are our
creator. We are your servants, O God,
and you are our master. We are your
body, O God, and you are our
intelligence.*

Ashanti, Ghana

7

GOODNESS AND PRAISE

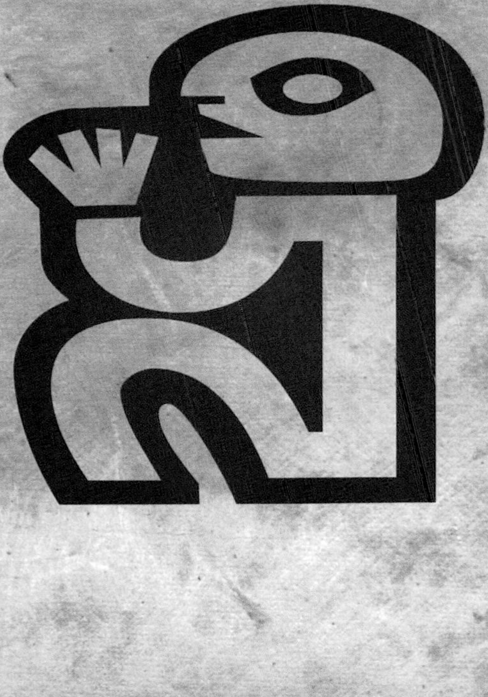

THE HAPPINESS OF INNOCENCE

You, O God, created all people. Let
my family always be happy. I have
not dishonored my father or my
mother. I have not committed
adultery. I am innocent of all sin. I
have stolen nothing. I have injured
no one without just cause. Grant
contentment to all who live in my
house.

Giur, Sudan

THE GUIDANCE OF ANCESTORS

We remember our ancestors, who
lived good and innocent lives and
now are dead. They are neither
blind nor deaf to our present lives;
they watch what we do and hear
what we say. May they guide us, that
we may live according to their
example.

Mende, Sierra Leone

LOVE AND HATE

*If I am hated, I hate in return. If I am
loved, I love in return. If a man comes
to rob my house or attack my family, I
shall ensure that he regrets what he has
done. If a man gives help to me or to
my family, I shall ensure that he rejoices
at what he has done. Am I right, O
God, to hate and love in this fashion?*

Dinka, Sudan

SNEEZING AND SLEEPING

*Thank you for the pleasure of sneezing,
which relieves my nose. Thank you for
the pleasure of sleeping, which revives
my limbs.*

Hottentot, South Africa

BEATING THE DRUM FOR GOD

I shall sing a song of praise to you,
O God; I shall beat the drum in
your honor. I shall sing of all the
good things you give us; I shall beat
the drum in your honor. I shall sing
of the beautiful women you have
made; I shall beat the drum in your
honor. I shall sing of the wisdom
you have taught us; I shall beat the
drum in your honor. Let the people
dance to the sound of the drum, in
honor of you.

Bakuba, Zaire

THE WORLD AS GOD WANTS

*Spirit of God, where you want
mountains, you pile up rocks with your
mighty hands; and where you want
plains, you crush rocks with your mighty
feet. Where you want lakes, you dig a
vast hole and fill it with water; and
where you want deserts, you send heat
to dry up every drop. Where you want
trees, you draw them out of the earth;
and where you want fields, you sweep
the earth clean. The world is just as you
want it to be. May we behave just as
you want us to behave.*

Shona, Zimbabwe

DIVINE JUDGMENT

You are the great God of heaven.
You are the shield of truth, the
tower of truth, and the sword of
truth. Against you no falsehood can
prevail. You sit in judgment on all
people. You know the thoughts, the
speech, and the actions of every
person; nothing escapes your notice.
And on the basis of your
knowledge, you determine whether
each person is righteous or wicked.
May my thoughts, speech, and
actions be counted as righteous.

Zulu, South Africa

SILENT AND INVISIBLE

*I honor you, for you are God. You gave
me my mother and father long ago, and
you gave me my wife and children. You
gave me my land and my livestock, and
you gave me the strength to work. And
you have shown equal generosity to all
people. Why do you keep silence? Why
do you not make yourself known? Why
do you not demand that people show
gratitude to you for your gifts? Even
though you are silent, I shall speak
loudly about you. Even though you are
invisible, I shall dance in your honor.
Even though you do not demand
gratitude, I shall never cease to offer
thanks to you.*

Shilluk, Sudan

REASONS FOR FAITH

We praise you because you are God and you protect us. We love you because you love us and embrace us. We honor you because you send rain each year and make our crops grow. We obey you because you reward good actions and punish wicked actions. We worship you because you fill us with joy and make us happy.

Hottentot, South Africa

INNOCENCE FROM GOD

O God, you have created all people to be good; and I have remained as you created me. I have not dishonored or offended my father or mother. I have been faithful and kind to my wife. I have cared for my children, teaching them the skills that they need for adulthood. I have never stolen any neighbor's possessions, nor blackened any neighbor's name, nor killed without cause. I am innocent, and my innocence comes from you.

Guir, Sudan

PRAISE FOR THE GOD OF ALL

God of our ancestors, we praise you.
God of our parents, we praise you.
God of our cattle, we praise you.
God of the sun that shines during the
day, we praise you.
God of the moon and stars that shine at
night, we praise you.
God of every creature that moves on the
earth, we praise you.
God of every plant that grows in the
earth, we praise you.
God of all, we praise you.

Masai, Kenya

BLESSINGS FROM THE GOD OF ALL

May the God of our ancestors bless
you. May the God of our parents
bless you. May the God of our
cattle bless you. May the God of the
sun that shines during the day bless
you. May the God of the moon and
stars that shine at night bless you.
May the God of every creature that
moves on the earth bless you. May
the God of every plant that grows
in the earth bless you. May the God
of all bless you.

Masai

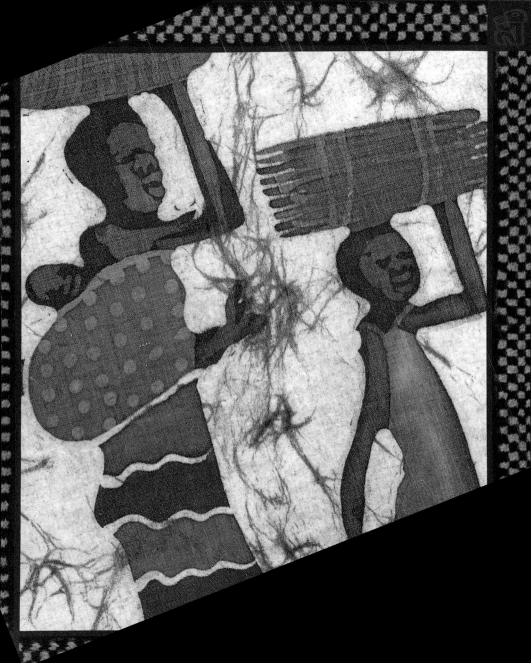

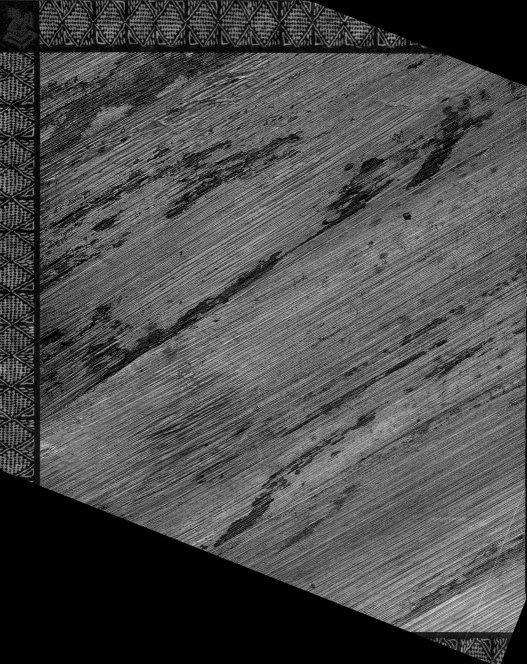

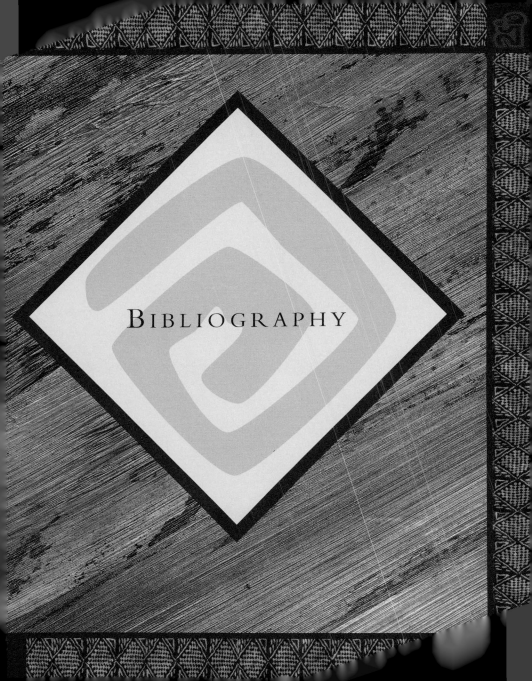

BIBLIOGRAPHY

Bibliography

This is a list of primary sources concerning African religion.

Beech, M. W. H. *The Suk; Their Language and Folklore*. Oxford, Clarendon Press, 1911.

Brown, J. T. *Among the Bantu Nomads*. London, Seeley, Service, & Co., 1926.

Campbell, D. *In the Heart of Bantu Land*. London, Seeley, Service, & Co., 1922.

di Nola, A. M. *The Prayers of Man*. New York, I. Obolensky, 1961.

Driberg, J. H. I. *The Lango, a Nilotic Tribe of Uganda*. London, T. F. Unwin, 1923.

Hollis, A. C. I. *The Masai; Their Language and Folklore*. Oxford, Clarendon Press, 1905.

Hollis, A. C. I. *The Nandi; Their Language and Folklore*. Oxford, Clarendon Press, 1909.

Mbiti, J. S. *The Prayers of African Religion*. London, SPCK, 1975.

Quatrefages, A. *Religion of the Hottentots and Bushmen*. London and New York, Macmillan & Co., 1895.

Rattray, R. S. *Religion and Art in Ashanti*. Oxford, Clarendon Press, 1927.

Roscoe, J. *The Bakitara or Bunyoro*. Cambridge, Cambridge University Press, 1923.

Routledge, W. S., & K. Routledge. *With a Prehistoric People*. London, E. Arnold, 1910.

Seligman, C. G., & B. Z. Seligman. *Pagan Tribes of the Nilotic Sudan*. London, G. Routledge & Sons, 1932.

Smith, E. W., & A. M. Dale. *The Ila Speaking Peoples of Northern Rhodesia*. London, Macmillan & Co., 1920.